IMAGES
of America

FORT ROBINSON

ON THE COVER: Prior to World War II, guard duty was an important part of every enlisted man's experience. In this photograph, members of the 10th Cavalry, one of the army's four black regiments, pose outside the guardhouse at Fort Robinson around 1907. During their 24-hour shift as guards, these soldiers had to remain in uniform so that they could respond quickly to any type of emergency that might arise on the post. (Nebraska State Historical Society, RG1517-2605.)

IMAGES
of America

FORT ROBINSON

Ephriam D. Dickson III

ARCADIA
PUBLISHING

ISBN 978-0-7385-5118-0

Published by Arcadia Publishing
Charleston, South Carolina

Printed in the United States of America

Library of Congress Control Number: 2007924174

For all general information contact Arcadia Publishing at:
Telephone 843-853-2070
Fax 843-853-0044
E-mail sales@arcadiapublishing.com
For customer service and orders:
Toll-Free 1-888-313-2665

Visit us on the Internet at www.arcadiapublishing.com

For Jennifer, with love

Contents

ACKNOWLEDGMENTS

This project would not have been possible without the encouragement of a number of individuals. In particular, I would like to thank Michael J. Smith, CEO and director of the Nebraska State Historical Society, who provided much-needed support for this project. Linda Hein spent many hours hunting up images, arranging for scans, and answering my many questions. I especially want to thank Tom Buecker, curator at Fort Robinson, for his continued encouragement and suggestions over the years.

INTRODUCTION

Since the advent of photography, the American West has been a favorite subject for many artists who traveled throughout the region creating images they hoped to sell to the public. Since its establishment in 1874, Fort Robinson has been the destination for a number of photographers, creating a rich visual heritage of the post. During the 1870s, with the Red Cloud Agency nearby, artists came to produce Indian portraits as well as outdoor scenes, while at the same time selling individual studio portraits to officers, enlisted men, and their families. Photographers such as Stanley J. Morrow, James H. Hamilton, D. S. Mitchell, and David Rodocker passed through the post during its first decade of operation.

Not all early photographers, however, were commercial artists. Lt. Thomas Wilhelm took up photography as a hobby and produced the earliest known images at the Red Cloud Agency in 1874. Pvt. Charles Howard, a soldier in the 4th Infantry, also enjoyed photography, landing a position on an army-mapping expedition that passed through the area in 1877.

Advances in equipment and film soon made photography accessible to the general public at a reasonable cost, and by the 1890s individuals could produce their own images. Surviving photographs suggest that they often chose subjects of personal interest—visual souvenirs of their experience at the post. Kate Hamilton, for example, was the young wife of 2nd Lt. George F. Hamilton. During the late 1890s, she captured on film various aspects of daily life at the military post and her home.

Despite the explosion of personal cameras, commercial artists continued to survive, often operating studios in larger communities. Following the establishment of nearby Crawford, several photographers maintained a studio in town where they offered professional portraits to soldiers and made occasional forays out to the fort to record buildings and events. Charles C. McBride was particularly prolific during this period. During the early 20th century, commercial photographers began to offer a new type of product—the picture postcard. These images highlighted buildings and experiences common to all soldiers in an effort to attract their purchase.

By World War II, the army recognized that public relations was an important element of its mission. Military photographers were sent to Fort Robinson at various times to record wartime functions such as the K-9 Corps. These images could then be distributed to the Associated Press or provided directly to newspapers in an effort to help communicate a positive image of army activities.

Whether a particular image was created for financial or personal reasons, together they provide a fascinating pictorial history of Fort Robinson. The images reveal how the military community developed over time. Today people can still explore this park, creating their own images of this historic place.

Red Cloud Agency. Oglala families gather outside the warehouse and bastion issue room of the Red Cloud Agency to collect their rations. The detail of this photograph is attributed to D. S. Mitchell, 1877. (Wyoming State Archives, No. 7758.)

One

The Frontier Years 1873–1879

American expansion onto the northern Great Plains brought the United States into conflict with the Lakota (or Western Sioux) tribe. In 1868, following three years of bloody fighting along the Bozeman Trail in eastern Wyoming, government representatives met with Lakota leaders at Fort Laramie to sign a new treaty of peace. The treaty set aside what is today the western half of South Dakota as the Great Sioux Reservation, as well as promised hunting rights in the surrounding areas, and established Native American agencies where food and other supplies could be issued to the Lakota. The Red Cloud Agency, responsible for distributing rations to the Oglala Lakota as well as to the Northern Cheyenne and Arapaho, was initially established in eastern Wyoming in 1871.

Despite the Fort Laramie Treaty, conflict with the Lakota continued as Americans became interested the Black Hills, located within the heart of the Great Sioux Reservation. In February 1874, following the killing of the agency clerk, the army marched to the Red Cloud Agency and established a military encampment known as Camp Robinson.

General Custer's expedition into the Black Hills in 1874 and the subsequent discovery of gold sparked a political crisis between the Lakota and the U.S. government. Initially the army attempted to keep the miners off the reservation while government officials tried to negotiate a new treaty. But after the treaty commission failed to reach an agreement with the Lakota, President Grant and his administration decided to launch a war against the "hostile" bands who lived off the reservation. The Great Sioux War of 1876–1877 compelled the agency headmen to sign another treaty giving up the Black Hills and forced the last bands of Oglala and Northern Cheyenne to surrender at the agencies, culminating with the surrender of Crazy Horse in May 1877. Four months later, Crazy Horse was killed at Camp Robinson during an attempt to place him under arrest. The Red Cloud Agency was removed to the Missouri River in the fall of 1877 and the following year relocated in Dakota Territory, where it became known as the Pine Ridge Agency.

Camp Robinson continued to operate as a frontier military post after the agency's removal. In 1878, the garrison was renamed Fort Robinson and participated in one of the final chapters of the Great Plains Indian Wars with the capture of Dull Knife's band of Northern Cheyenne.

DR. JOHN J. SAVILLE (1830–1910). A physician from Sioux City, Iowa, Dr. Saville was appointed as the new Indian agent for the Red Cloud Agency in 1873, just as it was being removed to Nebraska. He arrived at the new site to find no buildings had yet been constructed and his supplies piled under tarps. "I was left in a sufficiently embarrassing position to undertake so complicated a business," he later wrote. Despite his isolation and the sometimes rancorous politics, Dr. Saville did an admirable job. He finally resigned in frustration in 1875 following a congressional investigation. This photograph was taken in 1870 by B. H. Gurnsey in Sioux City, Iowa. (Nebraska State Historical Society, RG4341-7.)

RED CLOUD AGENCY ISSUING DAY. Soon after his arrival, Dr. Saville hired his brother-in-law Amos Appleton to oversee the construction of the Red Cloud Agency. The agency buildings included a large warehouse with an attached bastion, visible near the center of this October 1875 photograph. To the right is Frank Yates's store, one of two trading establishments authorized to operate at the agency. (Photograph by Albert Guerin; J. Leonard Jennewein Collection, Dakota Wesleyan University.)

DISTRIBUTING RATIONS. Dry goods such as flour, corn, sugar, and coffee were issued to each family every seven days. In this 1874 drawing, possibly by Jules Tavernier, Native American women can be seen inside the bastion presenting their ration tickets to the interpreters while agency employees in the warehouse weigh out a variety of rations for issue. (*Harper's Weekly*, November 13, 1875.)

BEEF ISSUE AT RED CLOUD AGENCY. In addition to the issue of dry goods, the agency staff also supplied Texas longhorn cattle as part of the Lakota's meat ration, as shown here in a photograph presumably by Pvt. Charles Howard in 1877. Initially the animals were turned loose from the corral and chased down in a manner similar to a traditional buffalo hunt. In later years, the beef was butchered by agency staff prior to distribution. (Nebraska State Historical Society, RG2955-34.)

Red Cloud (Mahpiya Luta, c. 1822–1909). Probably the best-known Oglala leader, Red Cloud was headman of the Itesica, or Bad Face Band, but his influence extended beyond his immediate camp. Red Cloud, shown here in 1877, was often viewed as the primary spokesman for all of the Oglala at the agency that bore his name. (Photograph by D. S. Mitchell; Smithsonian Institution, NAA 00210800.)

Young Man Afraid of His Horses (Tashunke Kokipapi, c. 1836–1893). Descended from a distinguished family of Oglala leaders, Young Man Afraid assumed his father's role as headman of the Payabya, or Pushed Aside Band, in 1874. Shown here in 1877, he was often a moderate voice between the various Oglala factions and was an honored leader who retained the respect of both the agency bands and the non-treaty bands during the Great Sioux War of 1876–1877. (Photograph by D. S. Mitchell; Larry Ness.)

RED DOG (SHUNKA LUTA, c. 1830–c. 1882). A Hunkpapa by birth, Red Dog married an Oglala and eventually became the primary spokesman for the Oyuhpe Band who had settled at the Red Cloud Agency. Red Dog actively recruited Lakota leaders to go to Washington, D.C., in 1875 to discuss the Black Hills issue. (Photograph by D. S. Mitchell; Nebraska State Historical Society, RG2955-13.)

LITTLE WOUND (TAOPI CIKALA, 1828–1901). Leader of the Kiyaksa Oglala, Little Wound was considered by officials to be the most influential headman at the agency. The Kiyaksa, or Cut Offs, was a coalition of smaller southern Oglala bands, numbering about 135 lodges or 960 people by 1877, the date of this image. (Photograph by D. S. Mitchell; Larry Ness.)

Blue Horse (Shunka Hinto, c. 1821–1909). Following the killing of his brother Big Mouth by Spotted Tail, Blue Horse assumed the leadership role of the Wagluhe or Loafer Band. He went to Washington, D.C., with Red Cloud in 1872, the date of this image, as one of the Oglala representatives from the agency. (Photograph by Alexander Gardner; Smithsonian Institution, NAA 06532500.)

Red Leaf (Wahpe Luta, c. 1812–c. 1895). A respected elder of the Wazhazha Brule, Red Leaf, seen here about 1872, and his band preferred to remain among the Oglala at the Red Cloud Agency. During the excitement in 1877, most of the Wazhazha left to join their Brule relatives at the Spotted Tail Agency. (Larry Ness.)

Dear's Trading Store. Indian trading stores were allowed to operate at the agency under a license granted by the Indian agent. Traders purchased the Lakota's cattle hides for between $2 and $3 in trade goods at their store, becoming a critical element of the native economy at the agency. After processing, the hides were shipped to tanneries in the East. Attributed to D. S. Mitchell, this photograph was taken in 1877. (Wyoming State Archives, negative No. 7757.)

John W. Dear (1845–1883). An ex-confederate soldier, J. W. Dear moved west after the war and became engaged in the Indian trade business, serving as one of two traders at the Red Cloud Agency from 1873 to 1879. Dear also started the first stage company to operate between Sidney and the Black Hills. This photograph was taken by Edric L. Eaton in Omaha, Nebraska, around 1875. (Fort Laramie National Historical Site.)

Frank D. Appleton (1850–1874). A nephew of Agent Saville, Appleton worked as the agency clerk until he was fatally shot in February 1874 by an unknown Oglala. Fearing further violence, Dr. Saville urgently called for troops to be stationed at the agency. Taken about 1870 in Sioux City, Iowa, this photograph is by B. H. Gurnsey. (Nebraska State Historical Society, RG4341-5.)

Col. John E. Smith (1816–1897). In March 1874, after marching 110 miles through snow, Colonel Smith arrived at the Red Cloud Agency with eight companies of cavalry and eight of infantry. His tent encampment was soon named Camp Robinson, named in honor of Lt. Levi H. Robinson who had been killed by a Lakota war party a month earlier. Colonel Smith is shown here a few years later in 1877 in a photograph by D. S. Mitchell. (Bradley Collection, Army Heritage and Education Center.)

Group at Dear's Trading Store. Identified here in 1874 are (1) Lt. William H. Carter, 8th Infantry, post adjutant at Camp Robinson; (2) Jules Tavernier, visiting artist from *Harper's Weekly*; (3) J. W. Dear, Indian trader; (4) Lt. James Buchanan, 14th Infantry; (5) Red Leaf; and (6) Willie Hunter, better known later as William Garnett, interpreter at the agency. (Photograph by Lt. Thomas Wilhelm; National Archives.)

Lt. Emmet Crawford (1844–1886). In October 1874, Dr. Saville attempted to raise a flagpole at the agency, creating an uproar among the Lakota. Lieutenant Crawford and 25 soldiers were sent to the agency, but it was the intervention of several influential Oglala leaders that prevented bloodshed. Lieutenant Crawford was later killed on the Mexican border, after which the newly established town near Fort Robinson was named in his honor. (National Archives.)

Camp Robinson, Nebraska. Initially established adjacent to the Red Cloud Agency, Camp Robinson was moved two months later to the mouth of Soldier Creek about two miles away, and construction of more permanent buildings began. In this 1875 view, the earliest known image of the post, the main garrison is surrounded by a low wall of cordwood. (Nebraska State Historical Society RG1517-13-04.)

Key to Buildings:
1. Commanding Officer's Quarters
2. Officers' Quarters (six duplexes)
3. Infantry Barracks
4. Cavalry Barracks
5. Workshops
6. Stables
7. Guardhouse
8. Commissary and Quartermaster Warehouses
9. Post Trader's Store
10. Hospital
11. Laundress Quarters

DELEGATION TO WASHINGTON, D.C., 1875. In an effort to persuade the Lakota to surrender the Black Hills, delegations were brought to the nation's capitol from all the agencies. Representatives from the Red Cloud and Spotted Tail Agencies included such men as, from left to right, (first row) Sitting Bull the Oglala; Swift Bear; Spotted Tail; and Red Cloud; (second row) Louis Bordeaux, interpreter at the Spotted Tail Agency; William Garnett, interpreter at the Red Cloud Agency; and Julius Meyer, owner of an Indian curio shop in Omaha. While meeting in Washington, Lakota leaders refused to sell the Black Hills. The government then sent a commission to the agencies to negotiate directly with the Lakota, hoping to bypass resistant leaders. This approach also failed to yield an agreement over the Black Hills. This photograph by Frank F. Currier was taken on May 13, 1875, in Omaha, Nebraska. (Union Pacific Railroad Museum.)

Brig. Gen. George Crook (1828–1890). When negotiations failed to yield the Black Hills, the army was ordered to launch a campaign against the non-treaty bands. General Crook, commander of the Department of the Platte, launched the first offensive in March 1876. During his second expedition that summer, he was pushed back at the Battle of the Rosebud, and while waiting for reinforcements, the 7th Cavalry was defeated at the Little Bighorn. This photograph of the general was taken by D. S. Mitchell in 1877. (Army Heritage and Education Center.)

William F. Kimmel (1842–1891). "They brag considerably about killing Gen. Custer and all of his men," the post trader at Camp Robinson, William Kimmel, wrote to his wife. "That was a terrible transaction and every red cuss in the country ought to be wiped out to avenge it." Kimmel sold his store the following year and returned home to Polk County, Nebraska. (Eleanor Kimmell Roubique.)

RED CLOUD (c. 1822–1909). In the fall of 1876, the army assumed control of the Red Cloud Agency, disarming the friendly bands and confiscating their ponies. When Red Cloud refused to move closer to the agency, a column of troops surrounded his village and arrested both him and Red Leaf. Shortly after Red Cloud's release, J. W. Dear helped photographer Stanley J. Morrow secure this portrait of the Oglala leader. (Smithsonian Institution, NAA 09851600.)

ORDINATION OF SPOTTED TAIL. In an effort to politically marginalize Red Cloud, the army appointed Spotted Tail as head chief over both the Red Cloud and Spotted Tail Agencies in October 1876. This action was largely ignored by the Oglala, and by the spring of 1877, Red Cloud had regained favor with most military officers. This photograph was taken by Stanley J. Morrow in 1876. (U.S. Military Academy.)

1st Lt. Charles A. Johnson (1840–1893). While most of the Lakota agencies were returned to civilian control in the fall of 1876, the Red Cloud Agency continued to be operated by the army until the summer of 1877. Lieutenant Johnson, 14th Infantry, served as acting agent at the time of Crazy Horse's surrender in May 1877. (Nebraska State Historical Society, RG 1652-1.)

Indian Agent James Irwin (1818–1894). Two months after Crazy Horse's surrender, Dr. James Irwin arrived at the Red Cloud Agency as the new Indian agent. "It now appears that Crazy Horse has not been acting in good faith with the Army," Irwin wrote soon after his arrival. "He has all the time been silent, sullen, lordly and dictatorial, even with his own people." (American Heritage Center.)

Iron Crow (Kangi Maza, c. 1849–1925). Leader of a small band of non-treaty Oglala, Iron Crow was among those who surrendered with Crazy Horse on May 6, 1877, the year of this image. Several months later, he traveled to Washington, D.C., with a delegation to meet with the president to discuss their future. That winter, however, Iron Crow and his band, discontented over the removal of the agencies, slipped away to join Sitting Bull in Canada. (Photograph by D. S. Mitchell; Nebraska State Historical Society, RG2955-3.)

He Dog (Shunka Bloka, 1840–1936). Also surrendering with Crazy Horse was his boyhood friend He Dog, leader of a small Oglala band known as the Cankahuhan, or Sorebacks. In this portrait taken in 1877, He Dog holds a three-bladed war club, a symbol of his position as a head *akicita*. He Dog also fled to Canada with the other Northern Oglala, who did not rejoin their relatives on the reservation until 1882. (Photograph by D. S. Mitchell; Nebraska State Historical Society, RG2955-7.)

LITTLE HAWK (CETAN CIQALA, *c.* 1835–1899) AND 1ST LT. WILLIAM PHILO CLARK (1845–1884). An uncle of Crazy Horse, Little Hawk was leader of the Hunkpatila Band of Oglala. Shortly after his surrender, he agreed to enlist in the army's Indian Scouts, commanded by Lieutenant Clark. In this 1877 portrait, Little Hawk wears an early peace medal, probably given to his grandfather during the Atkinson Treaty negotiations in 1825. "My grandfather gave me the medal when he died and told me to treat the whites well," Little Hawk asserted in an 1877 council meeting. "All of the fault is with the whites. I always remembered what my grandfather said." (Photograph by D. S. Mitchell; Smithsonian Institution, NAA 00209700.)

FRANK GROUARD (1850–1905). Serving as a scout and interpreter for the army, Grouard apparently mistranslated Crazy Horse's words during a council at Camp Robinson on August 31, 1877, setting into motion events that ultimately led to the Oglala war chief's arrest and death. Grouard is shown here in a photograph by D. S. Mitchell taken in 1877. (Missouri Historical Society.)

CAMP ROBINSON. An additional five companies of cavalry were quietly brought into Camp Robinson to aid in surrounding Crazy Horse's village and securing the leader's arrest. In the foreground of this 1877 photograph, a portion of these newly arrived troops can be seen occupying a temporary cantonment known as Camp Custer, located just south of Camp Robinson. (Photograph by Pvt. Charles Howard; South Dakota Historical Society.)

Lt. Col. Luther P. Bradley (1822–1910). Bradley was the post commander at Camp Robinson in 1877. "I wish some man of brains, with a little sensibility, could be in charge of the Indians for a year or two," he wrote in his diary, "with power to use the money appropriated by Congress for the best good of the Government and the Indians. . . . The Indians at Red Cloud and Spotted Tail are ready for this." (Photograph by D. S. Mitchell; Denver Public Library.)

General Bradley's Quarters, Camp Robinson. As Crazy Horse arrived at Camp Robinson on the evening of September 5, 1877, Bradley watched from the porch of his quarters. A request for a council that evening was denied. Instead, Bradley instructed that Crazy Horse was to be turned over to the officer of the day and taken to the guardhouse. (Photograph by Pvt. Charles Howard; Denver Public Library.)

LITTLE BIG MAN. A close associate of Crazy Horse, Little Big Man's own ambitions caused him to split with the Oglala war chief and ally himself with the agency bands. On September 5, 1877, he helped escort Crazy Horse into the guardhouse and was seriously cut when he attempted to prevent the war chief from escaping. (Photograph by D. S. Mitchell; Nebraska State Historical Society, RG2955-25.)

OLD PARADE GROUNDS, FORT ROBINSON. Inside the post guardhouse (right), Crazy Horse suddenly realized that he was being arrested and attempted to break free. He was fatally bayoneted by one of the members of the guard detail. Crazy Horse was then carried in to the adjutant's office (left) where he died later that night. This photograph was taken by Kate Hamilton around 1897. (Nebraska State Historical Society.)

Officers at Camp Robinson. Identified here in 1877 are, from left to right, (first row) Six Feathers, Arapaho scout; 1st Lt. Charles A. Johnson, Company F 14th Infantry; Capt. Deane Monahan, Company G 3rd Cavalry; unidentified civilian; 2nd Lt. Bainbridge Reynolds, Company F 3rd Cavalry; and Dr. Curtis E. Munn, post surgeon; (second row) 2nd Lt. Frederic S. Calhoun, Company F 14th Infantry and post adjutant, whose brother was killed at the Little Bighorn; Capt. Thomas F. Tobey, Company F 14th Infantry; 2nd Lt. James F. Simpson, Company G 3rd Cavalry; and 2nd Lt. James F. Cummings, Company L 3rd Cavalry. (Photograph by Pvt. Charles Howard; Denver Public Library.)

Oglala Delegation. One month after the death of Crazy Horse, a delegation of Oglala visited Washington, D.C., to talk about their future home. Identified here in 1877 are, from left to right, (first row) Yellow Bear, Joseph Merrival, William Garnett, Leon Pallardy, and Three Bears; (second row) He Dog, Little Wound, American Horse, Little Big Man, Young Man Afraid of His Horses, and Sword. (Photograph by Charles M. Bell; Smithsonian Institution.)

Red Cloud Agency. In October 1877, the Red Cloud Agency was moved to the Missouri River in Dakota Territory against the wishes of the Oglala leadership. Some of the original agency buildings continued to be used by J. W. Dear as a stage station along the trail to the Black Hills. This photograph was taken by David Rodocker, probably in November 1877. (Nebraska State Historical Society.)

Arapaho Leaders. While the Lakota were being removed to the Missouri River, the Northern Arapaho, shown here in 1877, were transferred to the Shoshone Agency in central Wyoming. (Photograph by Pvt. Charles Howard; Nebraska State Historical Society.)

LITTLE WOLF (LEFT) AND DULL KNIFE, NORTHERN CHEYENNE. The Northern Cheyenne surrendered at the Red Cloud Agency in the spring of 1877 and were shortly thereafter transferred to Indian Territory (present-day Oklahoma). The following year, a portion of the tribe under Little Wolf and Dull Knife fled north in a desperate attempt to return home. This photograph by Alexander Gardner was taken in Washington, D.C., in 1873. (Smithsonian Institution.)

CAVALRY BARRACKS. The Northern Cheyenne, with Dull Knife, were captured east of Fort Robinson in October 1878 and held under guard in the old cavalry barracks until they agreed to return to Indian Territory. The Cheyenne, nearly half of whom were killed in the ensuing fight, broke out of the barracks in January 1879. (Photograph by Kate Hamilton; Nebraska State Historical Society.)

MINNECONJOU SIOUX VILLAGE. Following the killing of Crazy Horse, the villages of Touch the Clouds and Roman Nose were moved closer to the Spotted Tail Agency, fearing they might slip away to the north. Taken in 1877, this photograph is by Pvt. Charles Howard. (U.S. Military Academy Library.)

Two

Camp Sheridan and the Spotted Tail Agency

Forty miles to the west of Camp Robinson stood a second, closely associated military garrison and Indian agency known as Camp Sheridan and the Spotted Tail Agency.

Established in 1868 on the Missouri River, the agency served as the distribution point for rations assigned to the Upper Brule, one of the major tribes of the Lakota. Over the next decade, the agency was moved six times, leading Spotted Tail to complain that his people had been "put on wheels." By 1874, the agency had been located on the White River at the mouth of Beaver Creek, northeast of present Chadron, Nebraska. Gathered here were several thousand Brule under the leadership of headmen such as Spotted Tail, Two Strike, Swift Bear, and Iron Shell.

Following the killing of the clerk at the nearby Red Cloud Agency, the army dispatched troops to guard both agencies. Four companies of infantry and two companies of cavalry were assigned to the Spotted Tail Agency, including Company C 8th Infantry commanded by Capt. A. W. Corliss. "Soon after our arrival at the agency, we looked about for a defensible position," Captain Corliss later recalled, "and finally occupied a hill near the river, where we erected two little redoubts for our Gatlings and built a line of rifle pits around our camp." Six months later, the agency and post were moved farther up Beaver Creek to gain better access to wood, but the fort's new location proved to have problems with drainage.

Capt. Anson Mills assumed command of Camp Sheridan in April 1875 and began construction on a new site near the agency. His soldiers also patrolled the area to intercept any miners attempting to sneak into the Black Hills. In May 1875, Captain Mills's command captured John Gordon's expedition, burning their wagons and placing its members under arrest. During the Great Sioux War of 1876–1877, troops from the post participated in several of the campaigns. Through the strong influence of Spotted Tail, the majority of the Brule remained out of the conflict. Spotted Tail led a diplomatic effort in early 1877 to induce the non-treaty bands to surrender, ultimately resulting in the surrender of many Minneconjou and Sans Arc, including the bands of Touch the Clouds and Red Bear.

In the fall of 1877, the Spotted Tail Agency was removed to the Missouri River. Camp Sheridan remained in operation for an additional four years but was finally abandoned in 1881.

SPOTTED TAIL AGENCY ON RATION DAY. In 1875, the Whetstone Agency was moved farther up Beaver Creek and renamed the Spotted Tail Agency in honor of the influential Brule chief. The agency, seen here about 1875–1877, included a warehouse, a house for the Indian agent, and a building for the Episcopalian church and school. (Minnesota Historical Society.)

BEEF ISSUE AT SPOTTED TAIL AGENCY. At the corrals along Beaver Creek, seen here about 1877, cattle were weighed and sorted by the agency staff in preparation for being issued to the Brule. These animals formed the most important part of the Lakota's economy at the time, providing meat for food and hides for trade. (Photograph by Pvt. Charles Howard; Princeton University.)

SPOTTED TAIL (SINTE GLESKA, c. 1823–1881). During the 1870s, Spotted Tail was the most influential headman of the Upper Brule, generally serving as their primary spokesman in talks with the U.S. government. His charismatic leadership kept the majority of tribe out of the Great Sioux War of 1876–1877, and he successfully persuaded a number of the non-treaty bands to surrender. His photograph was taken by James H. Hamilton in 1877. (Larry Ness.)

TWO STRIKE (NOMP KARPA, c. 1820–1914). Another leading headman at the agency was Two Strike, a longtime friend and associate of Spotted Tail. This 1877 photograph was taken by James H. Hamilton of the Spotted Tail Agency. (Sue Joplin.)

Camp Sheridan, Nebraska. Built on the eastern banks of Beaver Creek, Camp Sheridan consisted of more than 20 buildings arranged around a central parade field, as seen here in 1877. "The perimeter of the ground-plan is strangely like a coffin," Lt. John G. Bourke noted in his diary during his 1877 visit to the post. (Photograph by Pvt. Charles Howard; Smithsonian Institution.)

Key to Buildings:

1. Officers' Quarters
2. Adjutant's Office
3. Commanding Officer's Quarters
4. Guardhouse
5. Commissary Warehouse
6. Commissary Warehouse
7. Quartermaster Warehouse
8. Post Trader's Store
9. Barracks
10. Corral
11. Hospital
12. Laundress Quarters

Camp Sheridan, 1877. For his second view of the post, photographer Charles Howard moved up onto the bluff overlooking Camp Sheridan and pointed his camera east toward Beaver Wall. The back barracks and mess houses are visible, as is the post hospital. (Larry Ness.)

Adjutant's Office, Camp Sheridan. One of the original officers' quarters located at the head of the parade grounds was converted into the post headquarters, providing offices for the post commander and the post adjutant. Following Crazy Horse's escape to Camp Sheridan on September 4, 1877, he met with officers in this building to discuss his return to Camp Robinson. This 1929 image is a substitute for the original, which has since been lost. (*Nebraska History Magazine.*)

Capt. Anson Mills (1834–1924). As the commanding officer at Camp Sheridan in 1875, Mills oversaw the reconstruction of the post at its third and final location. He participated in the Great Sioux War of 1876–1877, including leading the initial attack on a village at Slim Buttes before returning to Camp Sheridan until May 1877. (National Archives.)

Capt. Jesse M. Lee (1843–1926). Serving as the acting Indian agent at the Spotted Tail Agency, Lieutenant Lee was present at the interview with Crazy Horse and agreed to accompany him back to Camp Robinson on September 5, 1877. At Camp Robinson, Lee watched helplessly as Crazy Horse was led off to the guardhouse, where he was fatally wounded moments later. (Fort Laramie National Historic Site.)

Grave of Crazy Horse. Four days after Crazy Horse's death, his aged parents brought his body back to the Spotted Tail Agency and placed it on a low scaffold, seen here in 1877, just opposite Camp Sheridan. "Whenever I go out of my quarters I see the red blanket in which his body is wrapped," Lieutenant Lee recorded in his diary, "and thus is recalled to my mind and heart Crazy Horse's pathetic and tragic end." (Photograph by Pvt. Charles Howard; U.S. Military Academy.)

Another View. Pvt. Charles Howard moved his camera to the opposite side of the scaffold and produced a second view of Crazy Horse's grave looking east. In late October 1877, when the Spotted Tail Agency was moved, Crazy Horse's body was taken by his family and buried—the exact location of which has remained a mystery to this day. (Larry Ness.)

TOUCH THE CLOUDS (MAHPIYA ICAHTAGYA, c. 1838–1905). Son of the prominent Minneconjou leader Lone Horn, Touch the Clouds, surrendered at the Spotted Tail Agency in the spring of 1877. On September 5, 1877, he accompanied his cousin Crazy Horse back to Camp Robinson and remained with the wounded war leader until he died late that night. "It is well," Touch the Clouds said as he laid his hands on Crazy Horse's body. "He has looked for death and it has come." (Photograph by James H. Hamilton; Sue Joplin.)

BRULE DELEGATION TO WASHINGTON, D.C. In October 1877, Spotted Tail (seated, center) led a delegation of headmen from his agency to meet with the president regarding their proposed removal. Despite their protests, President Hayes insisted that the Brule move to the Missouri River but promised that they could move again in 1878. (Photograph by Mathew Brady; Larry Ness.)

Fort Robinson, c. 1878–1879. An unknown photographer captured one of the last glimpses of Fort Robinson as a frontier garrison, just before construction began to expand the post. Nestled below the buttes near the head of the White River, Fort Robinson was considered by many visitors to be in one of the most scenic spots in the West. (Nebraska State Historical Society, RG1517-13-9.)

Three

FINDING A NEW ROLE 1879–1912

By the early 1880s, Fort Robinson's mission seemed increasingly uncertain as the frontier faded away and settlers began to arrive in northwestern Nebraska, establishing ranches and homesteads nearby. In 1886, the Fremont, Elkhorn and Missouri Valley Railroad was constructed through the post, and a second railroad was added nearby three years later. While many other western forts were being closed, the presence of a railroad meant that troops from Fort Robinson could be moved quickly to wherever they were needed.

Army officials began an ambitious program of rebuilding the post with more modern and permanent structures. A new parade grounds was established, and new officers' quarters and enlisted barracks were erected. Trees were planted, and wooden boardwalks replaced muddy paths. Gas lamps lined the streets, and homes soon boasted modern conveniences, such as plumbing and sewage disposal. A post theater and gymnasium were also built. By the turn of the century, Fort Robinson was among the army's most modern military installations.

In 1887, Fort Robinson was named as the regimental headquarters for the 9th Cavalry, one of four black regiments in the army. Buffalo soldiers from Fort Robinson were sent to the Pine Ridge Agency during the Ghost Dance troubles of 1890–1891 but otherwise endured the routine of garrison life. The new town of Crawford sprouted just off the military reservation, a rough western community offering a variety of distractions, such as saloons and brothels to off-duty soldiers. Racial tensions sometimes flared.

Following the Spanish American War, Fort Robinson became regimental headquarters for the 10th Cavalry, the second black cavalry unit, followed by the 8th Cavalry (1907–1910) and the 12th Cavalry (1911–1916). With its large wooded military reservation, the fort was well suited as a cavalry training area. During 1908–1909, Fort Robinson was extensively modernized with the addition of new brick quarters for officers and enlisted men. But as the 20th century began, the fort again faced the challenge of finding a new role within the changing mission of the U.S. Army.

Old Parade Grounds, c. 1886. The initial expansion of Fort Robinson included the construction of, from left to right, the new administration building (constructed in 1883) and the new post commander's home (built in 1884). In this view, new cottonwood trees have also been planted. (Nebraska State Historical Society.)

Log Barracks. The initial expansion of the fort also included the construction of new log barracks, completed in 1883. (Nebraska State Historical Society.)

FORT ROBINSON DEPOT. The Fremont, Elkhorn and Missouri Valley Railroad reached Fort Robinson in May 1886, opening a new chapter in the growth of the garrison. Troops could now be quickly moved closer to the reservations or elsewhere within the country if needed. (Nebraska State Historical Society.)

FORT ROBINSON. In 1887, Fort Robinson was significantly expanded. New adobe officers' quarters were added (upper right) as well as new enlisted barracks. The old portion of the fort (lower left) continued to be utilized, with several new structures added there as well. (Nebraska State Historical Society.)

OFFICERS' QUARTERS. Completed in 1887, the adobe officers' quarters were duplexes housing two commissioned officers and their families. Each family had a parlor, library, bedroom, bathroom, dining room, kitchen, and maid's room, offering more than twice the amount of space as the earlier 1874 quarters. (Nebraska State Historical Society.)

ENLISTED BARRACKS. For each company of enlisted soldiers, five barracks of adobe were built. Each building included a large open room for the soldiers' bunks and footlockers with an extension on the back for the kitchen and dining room. (Nebraska State Historical Society.)

OFFICERS OF THE 9TH CAVALRY. As the expansion for the post began, Fort Robinson was named as regimental headquarters for the 9th Cavalry, one of the famous "buffalo soldier" units. While the enlisted soldiers were all black, its leadership was initially composed of all white officers, as seen here in 1891. (Photograph by J. C. H. Grabill; Library of Congress.)

COL. EDWARD HATCH (1832–1889). After his distinguished service during the Civil War, Edward Hatch was named as the first commander of the newly formed 9th Cavalry in 1866. In 1887, he oversaw the expansion of Fort Robinson, where he died two years later following a carriage accident. (Army Heritage and Education Center.)

2nd Lt. George F. Hamilton (1870–1961). After graduating from West Point in 1894, Lieutenant Hamilton joined the 9th Cavalry at Fort Robinson until transferring for the Spanish American War in 1898. This photograph was taken by his wife, Kate, at Fort Robinson in September 1897. (Nebraska State Historical Society, RG4455-33.)

Lieutenant Hamilton's Quarters. In this rare interior view of an officer's quarters in about 1896, the mementos, musical instrument, and tea setting provide details of the couple's personal life. (Photograph by Kate Hamilton; Nebraska State Historical Society, RG4455-17.)

John Alexander (1864–1894). Graduating from West Point in 1887, Alexander was commissioned as a second lieutenant in the 9th Cavalry and arrived at Fort Robinson two months later. As the first black officer at the post, he found himself often excluded from many social events enjoyed by the white officers and their wives. (U.S. Military Academy Library.)

Charles Young (1864–1922). The third black officer to graduate from West Point, 2nd Lt. Charles Young was also assigned to the 9th Cavalry at Fort Robinson, leading some officers to complain that the regiment was being unfairly discriminated against. (National Archives.)

PALLBEARER'S AT COLONEL HATCHES'S FUNERAL. Senior noncommissioned officers of the 9th Cavalry pose in 1889. They are, from left to right, (first row) Chief Trumpeter Stephen Taylor; Sgt. Edmund McKinzie, Sgt. Robert Burley, and Sgt. Zekiel Sykes; (second row) 1st Sgt. George Wilson; 1st Sgt. David Badie; 1st Sgt. Thomas Shaw; and Sgt. Nathan Fletcher. (U.S. Military Academy Library.)

PVT. JOHN JEFFERSON (1878–1954). Grandson of the famous Black Seminole leader John Horse, John Jefferson enlisted in 1899 and was assigned to the 10th Cavalry. He served his second enlistment at Fort Robinson, where this photograph was taken in 1902. (New York Public Library.)

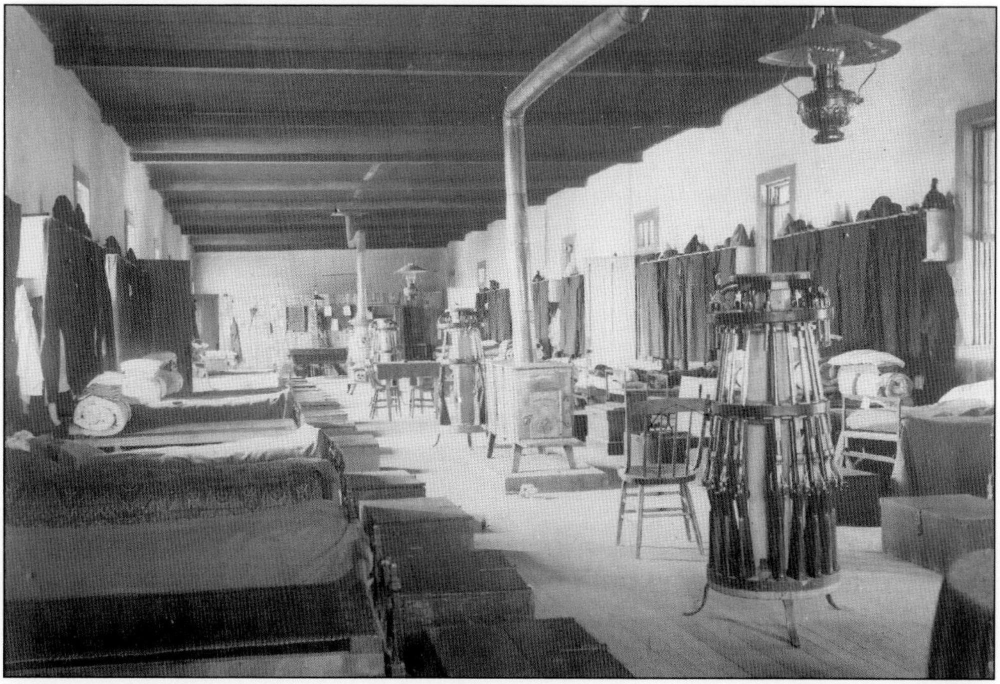

Barracks Interior. At the center of an enlisted soldier's daily routine were the barracks where he slept, ate, and socialized with other men from his company. Beginning in the 1870s, each soldier was provided his own iron bunk as well as a footlocker to hold accoutrements and a few personal items. (National Archives, RG92-F54-8.)

Barracks Mess Hall, c. 1898. An extension on the back of the 1887 adobe barracks housed the kitchen and mess hall for each company. Men were detailed from the company to serve as cooks, procuring food stores from the Subsistence Department. The company fund was often used to purchase additional condiments and special foods. (Nebraska State Historical Society, RG1517:56-3.)

Inside the Barracks. During their off-duty hours, soldiers often gathered inside their barracks to read, write letters home, or play cards. (National Archives, RG92-F54-7.)

K Troop Football Team. Athletics served as an important recreational activity for the soldiers at Fort Robinson. Teams from the post often played against local civilian teams. (Nebraska State Historical Society, RG1517:93-23.)

10th Cavalry Baseball Team. Composed of the best players from the regiment, the team was coached by Sgt. John Buck, seen here (seated) in a dark sweater. (*The Colored American Magazine*, 1905.)

Camp George Crook, Nebraska. During the 1880s, the army assembled troops from various posts to participate in an annual "camp of instruction," where soldiers received field training. Camp George Crook, held on Soldier Creek near Fort Robinson in 1889, was one of the largest with over 2,500 men from seven different regiments. (National Archives, 111-SC-82471.)

On Maneuvers. The wooded and rough terrain made Fort Robinson an excellent training area for cavalry. In this photograph by Kate Hamilton in August 1897, Troop I 6th Cavalry is seen riding near the buttes. (Nebraska State Historical Society, RG1517-PH-78-8.)

13TH CAVALRY. Mounted drill was a regular part of every cavalry soldier's routine. The 13th Cavalry was formed in 1901 and stationed at Fort Robinson until the spring of 1902. (Nebraska State Historical Society, 99184.)

8TH INFANTRY BAND. Even the regimental band participated in the army's camps of instruction. This photograph was taken near Fort Robinson about 1889. (Nebraska State Historical Society.)

PINE RIDGE AGENCY. Officers of the 9th Cavalry assembled for this group photograph, most likely taken by Gus Trager, during the Ghost Dance troubles in 1890–1891. (Denver Public Library, Z-6340.)

TROOP K 9TH CAVALRY. In 1890–1891, one company assembled at Pine Ridge, where three officers can be seen at left and 1st Sgt. George Jordan was awarded the Medal of Honor. (Photograph by Gus Trager; Nebraska State Historical Society, 100623.)

Mock Charge. With his saber drawn, an officer rides at the head of Troop I 10th Cavalry during a practice charge across the parade grounds at Fort Robinson. (Nebraska State Historical Society, RG1517:93-12.)

Reveille. Two soldiers from the 10th Cavalry fire the fort's salute gun for morning reveille in 1907. (Nebraska State Historical Society.)

POST HOSPITAL. Access to free medical care was another benefit of service in the army. A new hospital was built at Fort Robinson in 1884 with an additional wardroom in the white frame structure added in 1887. (National Archives, RG92-F-54-9.)

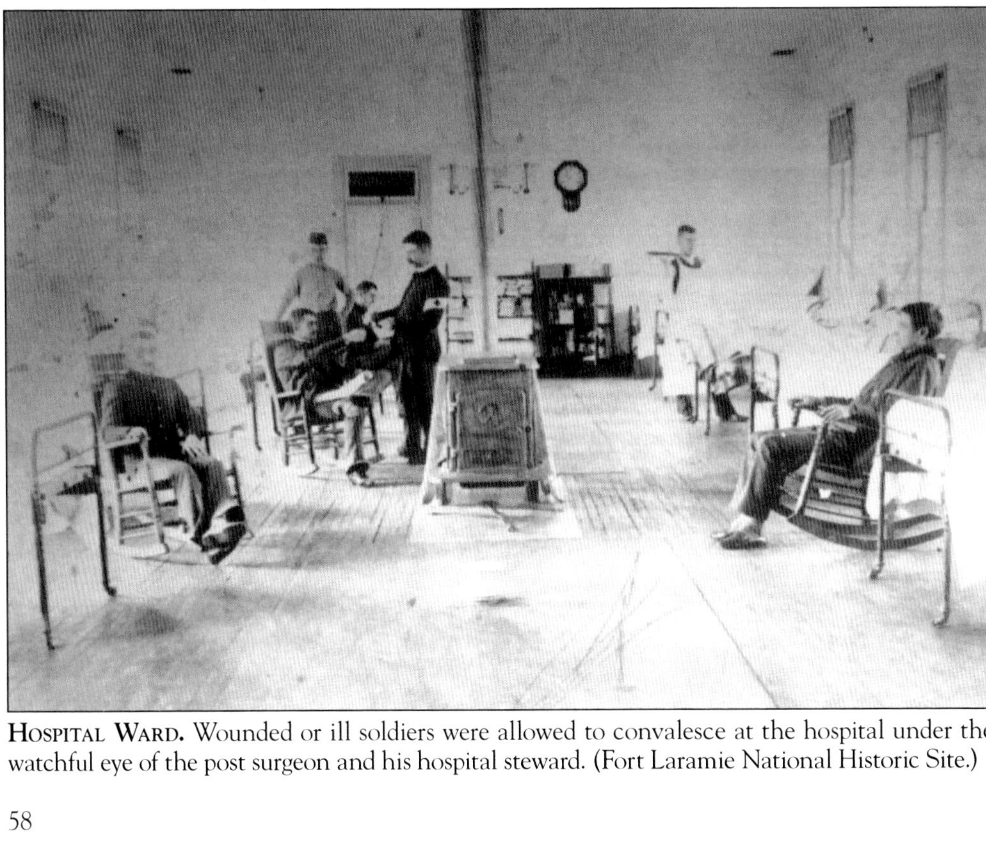

HOSPITAL WARD. Wounded or ill soldiers were allowed to convalesce at the hospital under the watchful eye of the post surgeon and his hospital steward. (Fort Laramie National Historic Site.)

View of Warehouse Area. By the late 1890s, Fort Robinson had expanded with the addition of new warehouses as well as a bakery, chapel, and guardhouse. This view was taken from the water tower. (Nebraska State Historical Society.)

View of Upper Parade Grounds. Also taken from the water tower, this photograph shows the addition of two new frame officers' quarters, a flagpole, and a bandstand. (Nebraska State Historical Society.)

WATER TOWER. Access to clean water was an important part of the fort's expansion during the 1880s–1890s, including the addition of modern plumbing and waste disposal. (National Archives, RG92-F-54-10.)

POST HEADQUARTERS. In 1905, a new post headquarters was constructed at one end of the upper parade grounds. In addition to providing offices for the post commander, adjutant, and other officers, the building also housed the post library. (Nebraska State Historical Society, RG1517:13-3.)

Post Commander's Quarters. As part of the post expansion in 1908–1909, a number of new brick quarters were constructed around the parade grounds for officers, including this spacious home for post commander. (Nebraska State Historical Society, RG1517:10-8.)

New Enlisted Barracks. In addition, two brick barracks were constructed, each housing two companies. In addition to large bay areas and kitchen and dining areas, the barracks included modern showers and toilets. (Nebraska State Historical Society, RG1517:117-27.)

In Dress Uniform. The army's new uniform, introduced in 1902, continued the traditional blue wool and a new cap for dress occasions. Here members of the 12th Cavalry pose on the front porch of their brick barracks around 1912. (Nebraska State Historical Society, RG1517:61-20.)

In Work Uniform. Men from Troop E 12th Cavalry appear in their new work uniforms of khaki wool with canvas puttees around 1912. (Nebraska State Historical Society, RG1517:54-3.)

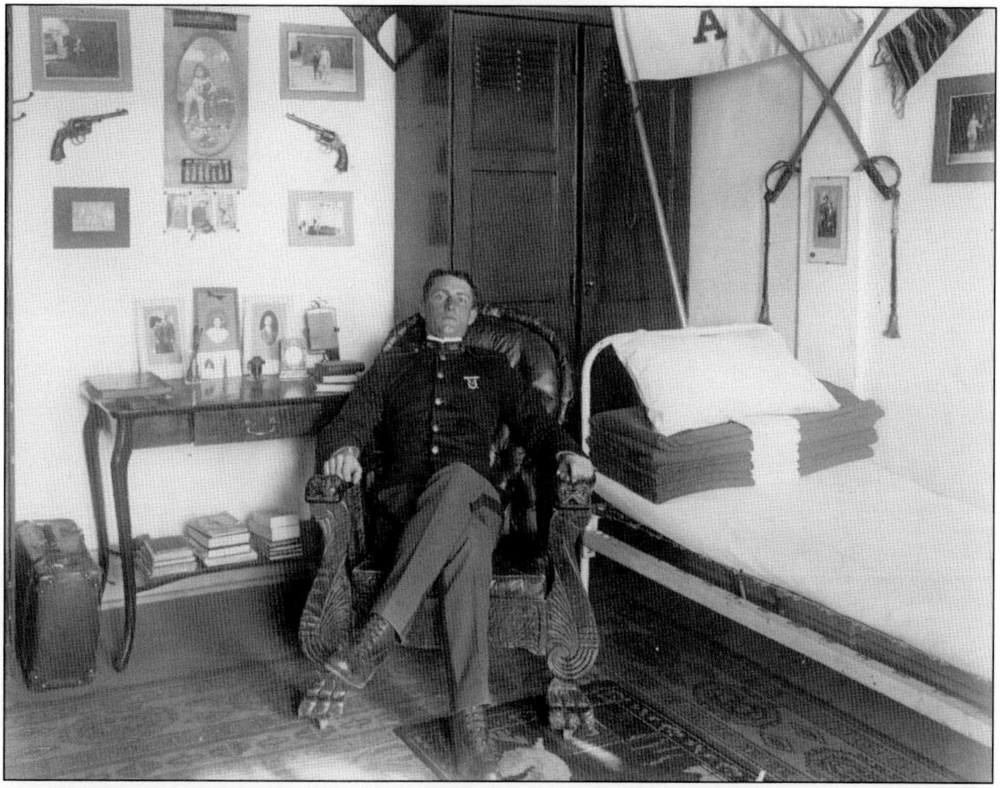

QUARTERS FOR CORPORALS, 1912. A benefit of serving as a noncommissioned officer was the privilege of some privacy. Cpl. Raymond S. Jones and Maurice G. Buchwald, of Troop A 12th Cavalry, have decorated their room with their guidon, weapons, and photographs of family. (Nebraska State Historical Society, RG1517:60-1.)

HIKE UP CROW BUTTE. Soldiers from Fort Robinson enjoyed recreation in nearby Crawford and on day excursions into the neighboring buttes, including climbing the famous Crow Butte. (Nebraska State Historical Society, 106901.)

Horse Jump Demonstration. Pfc. Ralph L. McClure at Fort Robinson demonstrates horse jumping over this fence in 1942. (Nebraska State Historical Society, RG1517-49-2.)

Four

Country Club of the Army
1919–1939

During the 19th century, procuring horses for mounted troops was generally left to each regiment, who assigned an officer to inspect and purchase animals from civilians. By the turn of the century, however, the army had become concerned about the quality of horses available in the civilian market and whether a sufficient number could be found quickly if the United States became involved in a large conflict. In 1907, the new Remount Division was established within the Quartermaster Department, centralizing the procurement process and establishing the army's own breeding and training program. Fort Robinson was selected in 1919 to serve as one of four remount depots where horses could be processed, soldiers trained, and the breeding program expanded. This opened a new chapter in the history of the post as it grew into the army's largest remount depot.

To prepare the fort for remount activities, the army constructed extensive corrals and shelter sheds, as well as miles of fencing. Animals were purchased from various civilian sources, including local residents, and shipped by rail to the fort where they were inspected, conditioned, and eventually issued to various units requesting mounts. The breeding program was also established. Veterinary clinics were held at the fort to help train local ranchers on new techniques, and stallions could be borrowed to help build up a reserve of good horses that the army could later purchase if needed. Beginning in 1924, Fort Robinson hosted an annual Quartermaster Day with animal exhibits, horse races, a polo game, and other festivities. In 1935, the army's Olympic equestrian team trained for the summer at the fort and returned for several additional summers until World War II intervened.

In addition to functioning as a remount depot, Fort Robinson also served briefly as an artillery post from 1928 to 1931. During the Great Depression, the Civilian Conservation Corps (CCC) was active at Fort Robinson, focusing on thinning trees on the military reservation and building holding ponds. By the 1930s, the improved quarters, availability of outdoor leisure activities, and the relaxed military atmosphere earned Fort Robinson the reputation as the "Country Club of the Army."

FORT ROBINSON. As part of the conversion to a remount depot, corrals such as the conditioning and issue area at the lower left of this photograph were constructed. (Nebraska State Historical Society, RG1517-49-2.)

FORT ROBINSON. In this 1934 aerial view looking west, the upper parade grounds and post headquarters are visible at the top, with the warehouse area in the lower center. (Photograph by Frank Snook; Nebraska State Historical Society.)

PURCHASING CIVILIAN HORSES. Purchasing officers of the various remount areas carefully inspected and measured horses before they were purchased for use by the army. (Nebraska State Historical Society, RG1517-45-31.)

HORSE N873. Records were kept for each horse purchased, often including official army photographs. Purchased in Oregon, this horse was classified as 7/8 thoroughbred and measured 15 hands, 2 inches high. (Nebraska State Historical Society.)

Arriving at Fort Robinson. After being purchased from any number of civilian breeders, horses selected for the army were sent by train to Fort Robinson for conditioning and training. (Nebraska State Historical Society, RG1517-45-47.)

In the Isolation Corrals. New horses were quarantined for 48 hours under the supervision of the veterinarian. (Nebraska State Historical Society.)

Dipping Vats. The horses were next run through a 60-foot-long dipping vat in an effort to control body lice and ringworm. (Nebraska State Historical Society.)

Interior of the Branding Chute. Here the newly arrived horses were clipped and branded. The irons were heated up in the furnace on the left, while the animals were branded in the chute on the right. (Nebraska State Historical Society, RG1517-22-1.)

AT THE FEED TRAPS. Horses were segregated into different pastures based on their age. (Nebraska State Historical Society.)

THE YEARLING PASTURE. Soldiers on horseback often helped to move animals between different pastures, as shown here on September 20, 1932. (Nebraska State Historical Society.)

FEEDING TIME. The remount horses were given a mixed feed comprised of ground oats, cracked corn, and bran. (Nebraska State Historical Society.)

FEEDING TIME. During the winter, the horses' diet was supplemented with prairie hay and alfalfa hay, cut by civilian employees from the fort or purchased on the open market. (Nebraska State Historical Society.)

UNLOADING HAY. Hay purchased by the army could be transported to the fort by rail. In this photograph, the freight cars sit on a rail siding at Fort Robinson until they could be unloaded and stored. (Nebraska State Historical Society, RG1517-45-42.)

MANURE DISPOSAL. By World War II, horse manure from Fort Robinson was being shipped farther west as ground cover at new military installations was being constructed in dry climates. (Nebraska State Historical Society.)

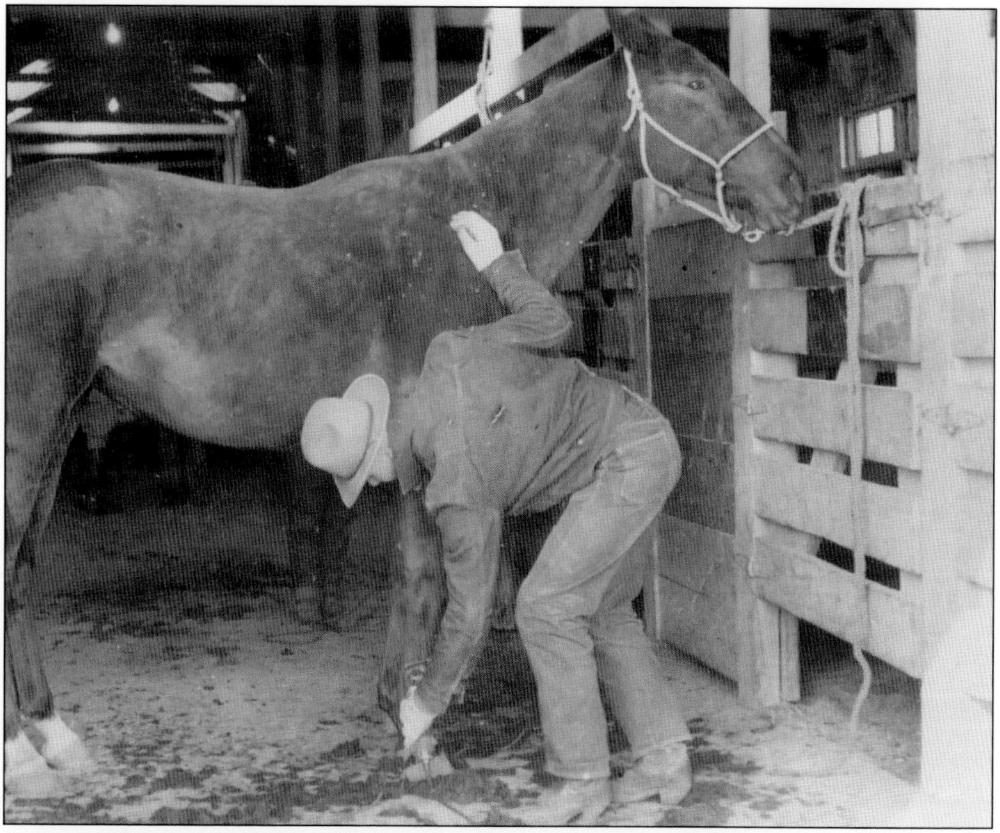

CHECKING HOOVES. Soldiers worked with horses until they were gentle enough to allow their feet to be lifted and cleaned. (Nebraska State Historical Society.)

RIDING OUT. After horses had completed their conditioning and training, they each had to be inspected by the training officer and remount depot commander before they could be certified for issue and then shipped out. (Nebraska State Historical Society, RG1517-45-33.)

VETERINARY HOSPITAL. Built in 1908, the veterinary hospital had to be significantly expanded to accommodate the needs of the remount depot. Additional stalls were constructed behind the building. (Nebraska State Historical Society.)

VETERINARY CORPS. The officers and enlisted men of the Veterinary Corps were responsible for monitoring the health of the horses at Fort Robinson. (Nebraska State Historical Society.)

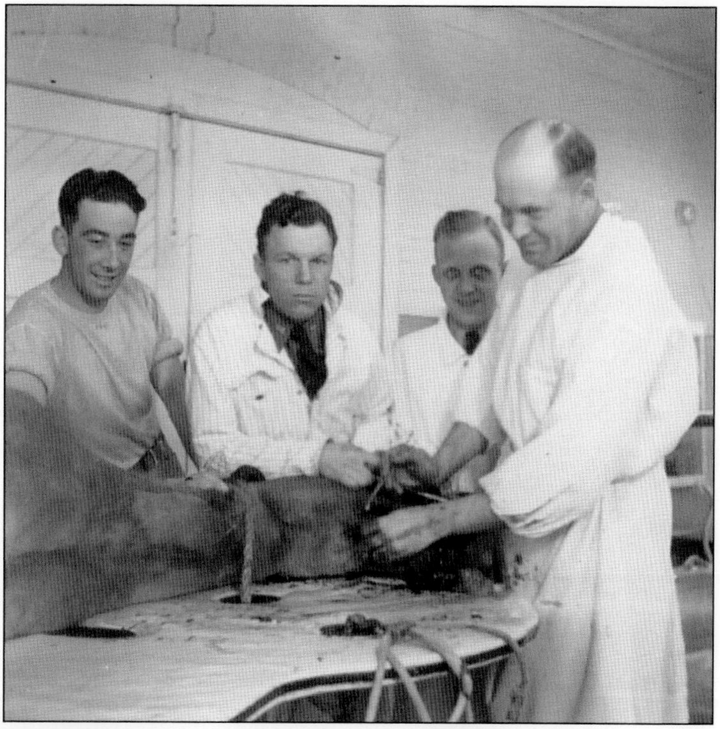

In The Operating Room. The staff of the veterinary hospital treated a wide range of ailments, most of which were related to respiratory issues. In 1929, the Veterinary Corps at Fort Robinson treated 633 horses and mules. (Nebraska State Historical Society.)

Field Care. Some surgical procedures were more easily accomplished outdoors. Here Maj. Clinton D. Barrett is shown removing a tumor from a horse with assistance from Pvts. H. Rounds and G. Richmond, standing at left. (Nebraska State Historical Society.)

Bud Parker (1893–1984). Transferred to Fort Robinson in 1924, Eric "Bud" Parker (left) was recognized as one of the best civilian horse trainers. He regularly rode on the polo and exhibition teams. (Nebraska State Historical Society.)

Barrel Racing. Cpl. M. J. O'Connell, riding Buckles, competes in the Bending Race on Quartermaster Day. (Nebraska State Historical Society.)

Pair Jumping Class. Cpl. Mike Jasmann (left) and Pfc. Weldon Harold (right) are shown side by side in pair-jumping class at Fort Robinson in 1944. (Nebraska State Historical Society, RG1517-45-28.)

U.S. Army Olympic Equestrian Team Training. In June 1935, the army's equestrian team arrived to train for the summer at Fort Robinson. This photograph was taken in August during one of the team's public exhibitions. (Nebraska State Historical Society, RG1517-49-2.)

On the Polo Field. Maj. Ralph G. Kercheval and Private First Class McLean override the ball close to the goal. (Nebraska State Historical Society, RG1517-50-1.)

Red Polo Team Champion. Shown on horseback, from left to right, are T/4 Rising, Captain Powers, Captain Hill, Staff Sergeant Jones. (Nebraska State Historical Society, RG1517-45-27.)

PREPARING FOR THE HUNT. The Soldier Creek Hunt Club was founded in 1932, and hunts were conducted twice a week. The post commander, Maj. Edwin Hardy (at far right), served as the master of the hunt. (Nebraska State Historical Society, RG1517-25-2.)

ON RIDE. Pleasure riding was also a common activity for officers, soldiers, and their families. (Nebraska State Historical Society, RG1517-47-5.)

Practice Firing. The 4th Field Artillery was assigned to Fort Robinson from 1928 to 1931. They found the rough terrain on the military reservation afforded great training opportunities. (Nebraska State Historical Society.)

Battery A in Position, Ready to Fire. A gun crew is in position around their Vickers-Maxim mountain howitzer. (Nebraska State Historical Society, RG1517-76-6.)

Sally the Gun Mule. The artillery piece came apart and could be packed on several mules for transport in rough terrain. (Nebraska State Historical Society, RG1517:64-11.)

Radio Operator. To coordinate firing, a radio operator receives the target coordinates from a forward observer, who then relays the information to the gun crew. (Nebraska State Historical Society.)

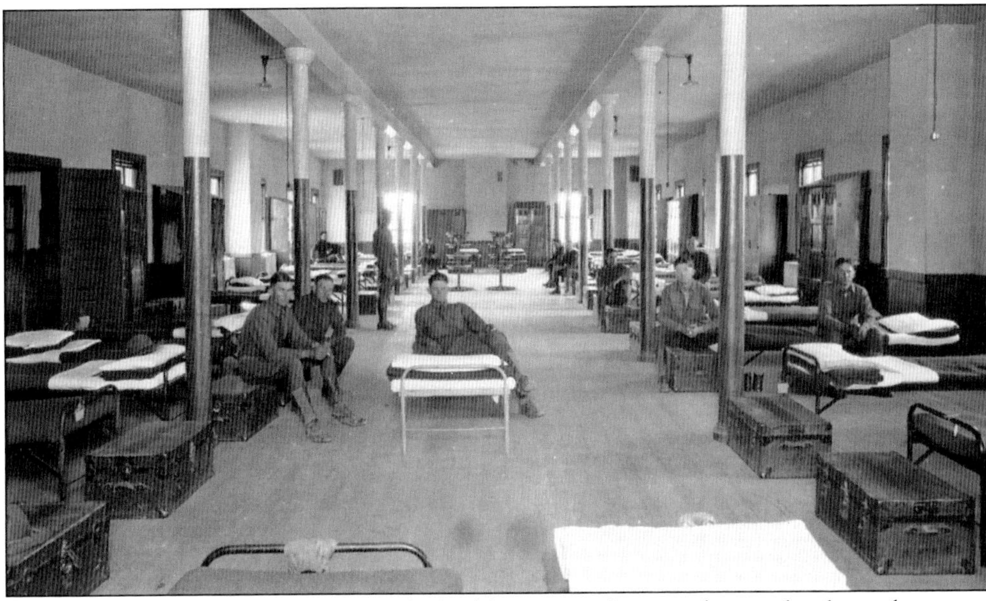

Squad Room. The newer brick barracks had larger squad rooms than earlier barracks, as can be seen in this c. 1928 view of the quarters for Battery A, 4th Field Artillery. (Nebraska State Historical Society, RG1517:84-7.)

Barracks Recreation Room. Using company funds, barracks generally supported libraries and recreational equipment, including pool tables and, in this case, a radio for members of the 4th Field Artillery around 1928. (Nebraska State Historical Society, RG1517:76-22.)

BAKING PIES. In the rear of the barracks, soldiers still worked in the kitchen cooking meals and washing dishes for the company. (Nebraska State Historical Society, RG1517:84-7.)

MESS HALL. Fourth Field Artillery enjoyed their meals together in the barracks' mess hall. (Nebraska State Historical Society, RG1517:84-11.)

Sawmill Camp. Built on a fork of Soldier Creek in 1933 to house a company of the CCC, Sawmill Camp consisted of two barracks, a mess hall, and a bathhouse/latrine. Camp supervisors had their own quarters. (Nebraska State Historical Society.)

CCC Mess Hall. Local pine lumber was cut on the Wood Reserve to construct the CCC buildings. The mess hall was also used for recreational activities. (Nebraska State Historical Society, RG1517:114-4.)

INSIDE THE CCC BARRACKS. Accommodations in the camp were rustic, with the young men sleeping on cots. (Nebraska State Historical Society, RG1517-114.)

CCC BOYS. Most of the young men who joined the CCC were between 18 and 25 years old. Each one was paid $35 per month and received an issue of army clothing to wear, including the blue denim and the olive drab shirts. (Nebraska State Historical Society, RG1517:114-6.)

Loading Up. Soldiers from Fort Robinson load into a truck as part of the basic training in 1943. (Nebraska State Historical Society, RG1517:74-01.)

Five

World War II

As the war commenced in Europe, public opinion was initially against U.S. involvement. Most army leaders, however, believed the United States' entry into the war was inevitable and so began planning, mobilization, and training. While security at Fort Robinson tightened slightly, daily remount activities continued as before. But everything changed on December 7, 1941, when the Japanese attacked the U.S. Pacific Fleet at Pearl Harbor. Lt. Robert McCaffree recalled how stunned he felt after first hearing the news on his neighbor's radio at Fort Robinson, "We could hardly believe it. We didn't talk much, just stared at each other." The country was now officially at war.

Remount activities initially began to increase, with over 3,000 horses and mules on hand at the beginning of the war. But development of modern weapons had already spelled the end of the horse-mounted cavalry and artillery in combat. Regiments soon began to mechanize. In 1942, for example, the 4th Cavalry came to Fort Robinson and exchanged their horses for jeeps and half-track vehicles. Fort Robinson's role soon shifted from procuring horses to now disposing of animals—feeding and caring for the herds until they could be sold at auction as surplus government property. Mules continued to have military importance as pack animals in areas with rough terrain. By the end of the war, as many as 500 mules were being conditioned and shipped out each month.

The U.S. Army reorganized its continental command structure, with Fort Robinson falling under the nearly created 7th Service Command, headquartered in Omaha. Because many of the remount soldiers had never been to basic training, a separate course was held for them at Fort Robinson in 1943. That same year, airborne troops used the fort for its war games. A detachment of the Woman's Army Corps (WAC) was also assigned to assist with various jobs around the post.

World War II brought a final period of building expansion at Fort Robinson. Temporary buildings were constructed for a variety of needs, including additional quarters and a new post exchange and recreational hall.

LAST HORSE-MOUNTED REVIEW OF THE 4TH CAVALRY. In 1942, the 4th Cavalry was ordered to turn in their horses at Fort Robinson in preparation for becoming fully mechanized. This was a difficult transition for some soldiers who had trained with their horses. (Nebraska State Historical Society, RG1517-45-48.)

VIEW OF THE STABLES. With fewer horses needed for the war, remount activities turned from purchasing animals to preparing them for auction, as shown here in 1943. (Nebraska State Historical Society, RG1517-45-48.)

Learning to Tie a Pack. While the number of horses at the depot declined, mules were in great demand as pack animals in difficult terrains. (Nebraska State Historical Society.)

Pack Mule Training, 1943. Mules were purchased and shipped to Fort Robinson, where they were conditioned and trained. The animals were exposed to artillery fire to simulate combat conditions. (Nebraska State Historical Society, RG1517:45-38.)

Close-Order Drill. Because a number of the remount soldiers had enlisted directly at Fort Robinson, many had never gone through army basic training. In 1943, these men dedicated their afternoons for six weeks to learn the basics. (Nebraska State Historical Society, RG1517:6-4.)

Combat Training. A martial arts expert was brought in from Denver to teach basic hand-to-hand fighting. (Nebraska State Historical Society.)

INFILTRATION COURSE. The most memorable part of the training was crawling through the infiltration course beneath barbed wire and machine-gun fire. (Nebraska State Historical Society.)

FIRING RANGE. As part of their basic training, soldiers also learned to fire the .30-caliber M1 Garand. (Nebraska State Historical Society, RG1517:6-3.)

FORT ROBINSON LANDING STRIP. To accommodate an airborne exercise, engineers from the Alliance Army Air Field came to Fort Robinson in July 1943 to construct a landing strip. In this view, C-47 transport planes wait to load the construction equipment for return to Alliance. (Nebraska State Historical Society, RG1517:88-1.)

PARATROOPERS LANDING. In August 1943, the "Battle of Fort Robinson" began with C-47s dropping gliders one day and paratroopers the next. Over 3,500 soldiers participated in the mock battle. (Nebraska State Historical Society.)

DANCE AT FORT ROBINSON. Social gatherings with the military and local civilians were a regular part of the post's community calendar. (Nebraska State Historical Society, RG1517:81-3.)

WEDDING. The post chapel was also the scene of a number of wartime weddings. (Nebraska State Historical Society, RG1517:95-5.)

Dog Sentry Duty. This guard stands at his post with his sentry dog at the Fort Robinson water towers in 1943. The war-dog program, or K-9 Corps as it was popularly known, initially trained dogs for sentry duty. Soon their role was expanded to include training as messenger, scout, and even mine-detection dogs. (National Archives, 111-SC-180119.)

Six

The K-9 Corps

In July 1942, the commander at Fort Robinson was notified that his post had been selected as one of two War Dog Reception and Training Centers to be established by the army. As the number of dogs used by the military increased during the war, a more intensive training program for both the animals and their handlers became necessary. As part of the Remount Branch of the Quartermaster Department, the center was responsible for selecting and training dogs and personnel for a variety of duties, including sentry, scout, messenger, and mine detection.

At Fort Robinson, an area just north of the warehouse district was selected for the center, and within a short time, training buildings and a canine hospital were completed. Individual kennels were also built, reaching a capacity of 1,800 kennels by the following year. Additional barracks and latrines were added later.

The first dogs and soldiers arrived in October 1942. "The sentry dog basic training was a two-week training program," Ralph Trickey recalled. After completing army basic training in 1943 at age 19, Trickey was transferred to the Reception Center at Fort Robinson to receive the specialized training for dog handling. "Basically, they taught us how to handle a leash, how to handle the dogs, how to feed dogs, how to groom them . . . I had one dog assigned to me for that two weeks." Most of the soldiers formed strong bonds with their animals. When Trickey returned from overseas, he was able to get an ownership transfer that allowed him to keep his dog.

Over the course of the four years that the War Dog Reception and Training Center was in operation at the post, an estimated 14,000 dogs were brought in and evaluated, from which nearly 5,000 successfully completed their training and were shipped out for active service in all branches of the armed services. The Fort Robinson War Dog Reception and Training Center closed in June 1946 after having made an important contribution to the war effort.

Arrival at the War Dog Reception and Training Center. The public donated their dogs through an organization known as Dogs For Defense, Inc., a group of breeders and trainers who helped to procure animals for the military. The dogs were then shipped to Fort Robinson in wooden crates, ready for the intake process. (Nebraska State Historical Society, RG1517-52-38.)

Dog Receiving Distemper Serum, 1943. After arriving at Fort Robinson, all donated dogs underwent a physical exam and were given shots for rabies and distemper. If the dogs passed their inspections, they were isolated for two weeks prior to beginning their training. (National Archives, 111-SC-180118.)

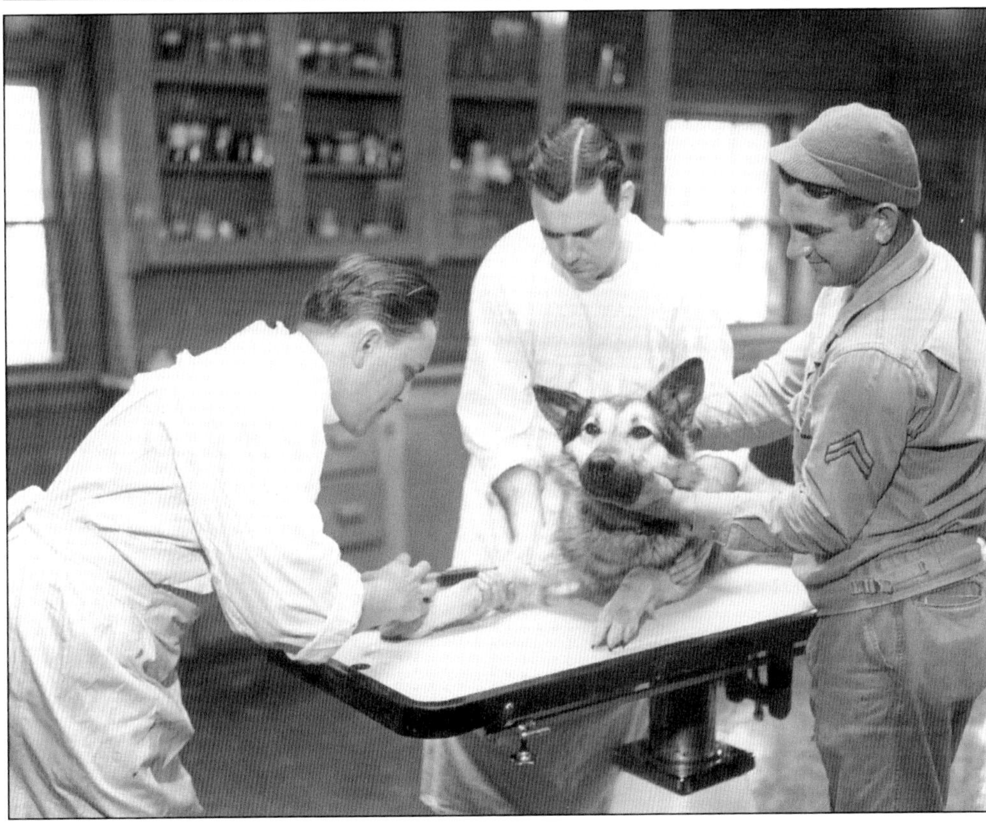

Veterinary Staff. Building No. 114, constructed in 1942, was the canine hospital that was staffed by a full veterinary crew. Pictured from left to right are Capt. Joseph J. Meranda, veterinarian; S.Sgt. John R. Rodemon, hospital clerk; Lt. Howard J. Cleveland, veterinarian; Cal Smith, clerk; John G. Donnelle; Capt. Wilber H. Mowder, veterinarian; and Col. Clinton D. Barrett, chief veterinarian. (Nebraska State Historical Society.)

"Boy" on His Kennel, 1943. Each dog lived in its own 4-foot-by-4-foot kennel, to which was tethered by a 9-foot-long chain. (National Archives, 111-SC-180120.)

KENNEL AREA. The entire kennel area was divided into sections of 96 kennels each. This arrangement greatly facilitates control of all operations—feeding, watering, training, care of the sick, and so forth. (Nebraska State Historical Society, RG1517-52-36.)

KENNEL POLICE. Each dog kennel was constructed with a hinged roof to aid in cleaning. Part of a soldier's daily duty was to clean his dog's kennel area to help ensure animals remained healthy. (National Archives, 111-SC-180117.)

Meal Time. Dogs were fed once a day at 4 p.m., their ration consisting of a mixture of horse meat, corn meal, and commercial dog food. Area residents recall hearing the excited barking of the numerous dogs miles away as the feeding wagon approached the kennel area. (National Archives, 111-SC-180116.)

Cleaning Up. After a reasonable length of time for the dogs to eat, the feed pans were collected and returned to the kitchen for a thorough scrubbing before the next day's meal. (Nebraska State Historical Society, RG1517-52-30.)

Lester Gertsch and His Dog, Major, at Fort Robinson. Each soldier arriving at the War Dog Reception and Training Center was matched with one or more dogs for the training course. During its first two years of operation, the War Dog Reception and Training Center graduated nearly 2,000 men as dog handlers, most from the U.S. Army and Coast Guard. (Nebraska State Historical Society.)

A War-Dog Platoon. By 1944, the center shifted from training individual soldiers and their sentry dogs to training integrated war-dog platoons. Commanded by a lieutenant, each platoon consisted of about 20 soldiers, 18 scout dogs, and six messenger dogs. Most were deployed to the Pacific, where they were used to locate and identify the enemy in combat zones. (Nebraska State Historical Society, RG1517-52-60.)

Running the Obstacle Course. An important part of every dog's training and conditioning was the obstacle course, known locally as the "Crazy Horse Run." In this photograph, the handler and his dog are shown pursuing an "agitator" through the stumps obstacle and across a 3-foot jump. (National Archives, SC-111-180113.)

Obedience Training. During the early part of the training, the dogs also learned to follow basic commands, such as "sit" and "come," as illustrated in this photograph of Coast Guard handlers and their dogs. Several of the new temporary barracks, built during the winter of 1942–1943, can be seen in the background. (Nebraska State Historical Society.)

Training Guard Dogs. Some dogs were trained to react aggressively toward strangers. The army handler had to learn how to properly control the dog, working as a team in the field. (Nebraska State Historical Society, RG1517-52-40.)

Dog Attacks. To teach a dog to attack from the rear was the goal of attack training. A mouthful of teeth in the upper arm was generally enough to make any intruder drop a gun or knife. (National Archives, 111-SC-180114.)

K-9 TRAINING. Soldiers worked long hours with their dogs, establishing trust and understanding. In the background, the large training shed can be seen where work continued even in bad weather. (Nebraska State Historical Society.)

ON PARADE. The training of the soldier-dog team also included close-order drills, seen here on the edge of the K-9 area at Fort Robinson around 1944. (Nebraska State Historical Society.)

PREPARING TO LEAVE. With their training complete, the war dogs were packed into shipping crates and left by train for their first duty station. (Nebraska State Historical Society.)

ON THE BARRACKS PORCH. The war-dog training program was operated by the K-9 detachment, composed of soldiers and officers assigned to the post either in administration or training. (Nebraska State Historical Society.)

K-9 FIRST SERGEANT. M.Sgt. William L. Ober served as first sergeant for the K-9 Corps at Fort Robinson. (Nebraska State Historical Society.)

K-9 HEADQUARTERS OFFICE STAFF. The clerical staff maintained detachment records, filled out shipping records, and submitted monthly status reports. From left to right are (first row) Faye Mary, unidentified, Jean Drinkwalter, Doris Rawalt, Jean Maunier, and Bonnie Royal Halloway; (second row) Jim Hugives, unidentified, J. C. Ferguson, and Fred Huber. (Nebraska State Historical Society, RG 2452.)

HEADQUARTERS, PRISONER-OF-WAR CAMP. The flag in the background is flying at half-mast for President Roosevelt's death in April 1945. (Nebraska State Historical Society, RG4889:1-5.)

Seven

Prisoner-of-War Camp

In the fall of 1942, the United States agreed to assist Great Britain with the tens of thousands of German and Italian prisoners captured during the war. Over the next two years, nearly 400 prisoner-of-war (POW) camps were constructed throughout the United States, ultimately housing over 425,000 prisoners by the end of the war.

Fort Robinson was one of the sites selected for a POW camp. Built near the old Red Cloud Agency, the camp was originally designed to house 1,000 prisoners, but its capacity was soon expanded to over 3,000. Construction began in December 1942 and was completed by the fall of 1943. The POW camp included three adjacent compounds, each to house four companies. A garrison area was also constructed on the north side for the soldiers who operated the camp. Staffing included a headquarters company, the 1765th Service Unit, and two military police companies, the 331st and the 635th. In November 1943, the first prisoners arrived: 680 German soldiers captured from the 10th Panzer Division in General Rommel's famous Afrika Korps.

The prisoners worked at various chores around Fort Robinson under the close supervision of military guards. Some were employed in the remount areas, helping to feed horses and clean stables. Others assisted with building maintenance, road repair, and fence construction. Each prisoner received a voucher for 10¢ for each day worked that could be spent in the canteen on items such as cigarettes, candy, and toiletries.

Recreational activities were also an important part of the POW experience. Soccer was especially popular, as were volleyball, baseball, and handball. Educational courses, including both informal classes and college-level correspondence classes, were offered at the camp. Movies were shown regularly, and religious services were conducted on Sundays. The German Red Cross helped establish a library for the prisoners. Initially German soldiers were allowed to display Nazi flags and portraits of Adolph Hitler in their barracks; however, in the final years of the camp's operation, more intensive reeducation programs were undertaken and all pro-Nazi material was removed.

The Fort Douglas Prisoner of War Camp reached its peak in February 1945 with just over 3,000 prisoners. As the war ended, prisoners were gradually transferred out and eventually sent home. The camp officially closed in May 1946.

VIEW OF THE ADMINISTRATIVE AREA. Buildings for the military police and administrative offices were located at the north end of the POW camp. Visible in this photograph taken from one of the guard towers about 1944 are the (1) officers club, (2) mess hall, (3) fire station, and (4 and 5) officers' quarters. (Nebraska State Historical Society, RG1517-115-05.)

COL. ARTHUR C. BLAIN (1892–1969). Son of an influential Georgia doctor, Colonel Blain received his commission as a second lieutenant in the infantry in 1918. Described as "rugged yet courteous," he served as commander of the POW camp from February 1944 through the end of the war. This photograph by Alfred A. Thompson was taken outside the camp headquarters building in August 1944. (Nebraska State Historical Society, RG2725-28.)

ALTERNATE VIEW OF THE ADMINISTRATIVE AREA. In this second photograph taken from one of the guard towers, additional buildings at the interment camp are visible, including the (1) NCO Club, (2) headquarters building, (3) post exchange, (4) guardhouse, (5) barracks for the guard, and (6) warehouse. Crow Butte can be seen in the background. (Nebraska State Historical Society.)

ALFRED A. THOMPSON (1918–1994). Thompson served as the intelligence officer at the POW camp and was one of the few individuals allowed to have a camera inside. The majority of the photographs in this section were taken by him. (Nebraska State Historical Society, RG2725-26.)

Camp Administration. With a map of the camp on the wall behind him, this unidentified sergeant works at his desk in the administrative offices of the POW camp around 1944. (Photograph by Alfred A. Thompson; Nebraska State Historical Society, RG2725-31.)

Sgt. Samuel L. Mitchell. Understanding that the prisoners at Fort Robinson were to be Italian, Sergeant Mitchell recalled taking an Italian-language class. The first prisoners, however, were German. (Nebraska State Historical Society, RG4001-54.)

Dr. John C. McGalliard (1906–1993). Seated on his bunk inside the guard company barracks, Dr. McGalliard served as an interpreter at the POW camp. With a Ph.D. from Harvard University, he spoke multiple languages. After the war, Dr. McGalliard returned to teaching at the University of Iowa, where he was a respected medieval literature scholar. (Nebraska State Historical Society, RG4001-51.)

Mess Hall. Two military police units, the 331st and 635th, provided security for the camp, while the 1765th Service Unit was responsible for administration. (Nebraska State Historical Society.)

New Prisoners Arrive, October 1944. Upon their arrival at the camp, all prisoners were searched, given a medical exam, and photographed. They were then assigned to a prisoner company. (Photograph by Alfred. A. Thomson; Nebraska State Historical Society, RG2725-14.)

"PW" At Work. Each prisoner was issued clothing stamped with the letters *P* and *W* to distinguish them. The truck in the background bears a seven-pointed star, the emblem of the 7th Service Command. (Nebraska State Historical Society, RG1517:59-6.)

General View of POW Camp, April 1945. Six guard towers marked the edges of the prison compounds, each equipped with a searchlight, siren, and .30-caliber machine gun. (Photograph by Alfred A. Thompson; Nebraska State Historical Society, RG2725-2.)

Prison Compound. On the right edge of this photograph, just inside the main fence, a single wire called the "dead line" can be seen. Prisoners crossing this wire could be fired upon by the tower guards. (Nebraska State Historical Society.)

KITCHEN STAFF AT CAMP, AUGUST 1944. The prisoners worked at various tasks in their camp, such as cleaning and cooking. (Nebraska State Historical Society, RG4001-52.)

SOCCER GAME, OCTOBER 1944. A variety of activities were available for the prisoners, including soccer, which was played in the recreation area within the fenced compound. By 1944, nine soccer teams had been established in the camp. (Photograph by Alfred A. Thompson; Nebraska State Historical Society, RG2725-24.)

A Prisoner of War Show. One of the buildings served as a theater known as Varista Hall, short for Variete im Stacheldraht or Variety in Barbed Wire. (Nebraska State Historical Society, RG2527-15.)

Crazy Horse Monument. Erected in 1934 behind the post headquarters, this stone pyramid commemorates the famed Oglala war leader Crazy Horse, who was killed at Fort Robinson in 1877. (Nebraska State Historical Society.)

Eight

Preserving the Past

During the early 20th century, interest began to grow in commemorating the events and places connected to the American West, including Fort Robinson. In 1913, soldiers from the fort were used as extras in Buffalo Bill Cody's film about Wounded Knee. Four years later, a large gathering of Lakota was organized in the Crawford City Park to dedicate a marble monument about the Black Hills Treaty negotiations. Other monuments were erected in the 1930s.

The largest commemorative event at Fort Robinson came in September 1934. The post commander, Maj. Edwin N. Hardy, used army funds to erect two large stone pyramids immediately behind the post headquarters. One was dedicated to Lt. Levi H. Robinson, killed by the Lakota in 1874 and for whom the post was named. The second was for the famous Oglala war leader, Crazy Horse, who had surrendered at the post in 1877 and was killed during an attempt to arrest him. Invitations to the Pine Ridge and Rosebud Reservations drew nearly 1,200 Lakota for the ceremony. Hundreds of residents and tourists also came out for the three-day event, billed as "The Last Great Gathering of the Sioux Nation."

As the U.S. Army demobilized at the end of World War II, Fort Robinson began to close down its remount and other wartime operations. In 1948, the post was officially turned over to the U.S. Department of Agriculture (USDA) to be used as a beef cattle research station. Concerned about maintaining so many buildings on their limited budget, USDA officials proposed the demolition of 94 structures, creating an outcry from the local community.

In 1955, the Nebraska State Historical Society was granted permission to establish a museum at Fort Robinson and the Nebraska Game, Forestation, and Parks Commission was given the original row of adobe officers' quarters for use as tourist cabins. Conflicts over joint use of the property ultimately led to the transfer of Fort Robinson to the State of Nebraska in 1972. The fort now began its new role as a state historic site and recreational park.

MONUMENT DEDICATION. The largest historical gathering occurred in September 1934 when Maj. Edwin Hardy, post commander, erected two stone monuments, one for Lt. Levi Robinson and the other for Crazy Horse, each representing the two sides of the conflict during the period. Three days of activities drew thousands of participants and spectators, including over 1,200 Lakota from the reservations. (Nebraska State Historical Society.)

The Ceremony. Decorated with flags and Native American artifacts, the back porch of the post headquarters building served as the central stage and podium for various speakers during the 1934 ceremony. (Nebraska State Historical Society.)

From the Reservation. Among the Lakota who gathered for the 1934 celebration were, from left to right, (first row) John Red Bear, Bear Dog, Eagle Bear, Joseph High Eagle, Bad Wound, and Martin Red Bear; (second row) unidentified, Rose Ecoffey, Henry Fielder (interpreter), Julia Red Bear, Turning Bear, Thick Shirt (Thomas Henry), Black Spotted Horse, Brave Bird, and Major Edwin Hardy. (Nebraska State Historical Society, RG1517:90-11.)

FROM THE RESERVATION. Also gathered for the 1934 celebration were, from left to right, (first row) Left Heron, Drags Rope, White Bull No. 2, Silas Yellow Boy, and Henry Yellow Shield; (second row) Black Horn, Major General Louis H. Bash, Jim Red Cloud, James H. Cook, Silas Fills Pipe, Eagle Road, Susie Yellow Boy, and Iron Shell. (Nebraska State Historical Society, RG1517:90-11.)

THE 1905 POST HEADQUARTERS BUILDING. Remodeled and reopened in 1956 as the new Fort Robinson Museum, the post headquarters building houses exhibits that tell the story of the garrison's history. (Nebraska State Historical Society.)

EXCAVATION OF THE 1874 CAVALRY BARRACKS. The first post guardhouse and the headquarters building were both excavated and reconstructed in 1966–1967. More recently, the Nebraska State Historical Society uncovered the site of the 1874 cavalry barracks. In 2003, the reconstruction of this building was completed, giving visitors an additional glimpse of early post history.

Vance E. Nelson, 1980. Serving as the curator at the Fort Robinson Museum for 20 years, from 1965 to 1985, former schoolteacher Vance Nelson emphasized interpretive programs at the park, including school field days and living history interpretations. His wife, Karen, was also a frequent participant. (Photograph by E. Dickson.)

THOMAS R. BUECKER, 2001. Buecker became curator at the Fort Robinson Museum in 1985. Over the next two decades, Buecker wrote numerous historical articles and produced a definitive two-volume history of the post. He and other society staff also host a regular military history symposium at the fort. (Photograph by Donald Cunningham.)

BIBLIOGRAPHY

Bray, Kingsley. *Crazy Horse: A Lakota Life*. Norman, OK: University of Oklahoma Press, 2006.

Buecker, Thomas R. *Fort Robinson and the American West, 1874–1899*. Lincoln, NE: Nebraska State Historical Society, 1999.

———. *Fort Robinson and the American Century, 1900–1948*. Lincoln, NE: Nebraska State Historical Society, 2002.

——— and R. Eli Paul. *The Crazy Horse Surrender Ledger*. Lincoln: Nebraska State Historical Society, 1994.

Carter, William H. *The History of Fort Robinson, Nebraska*. Crawford, NE: Northwest Nebraska News, 1942.

Grange, Roger T. "Fort Robinson: Outpost on the Plains," *Nebraska History* 39 (Sept. 1959): 191–241.

Hyde, George E. *Red Cloud's Folk*. Norman, OK: University of Oklahoma Press, 1937.

Olson, James C. *Red Cloud and the Sioux Problem*. Lincoln, NE: University of Nebraska Press, 1965.

Schubert, Frank N., *Outpost of the Sioux Wars: A History of Fort Robinson*. Lincoln, NE: University of Nebraska Press, 1995.

INDEX

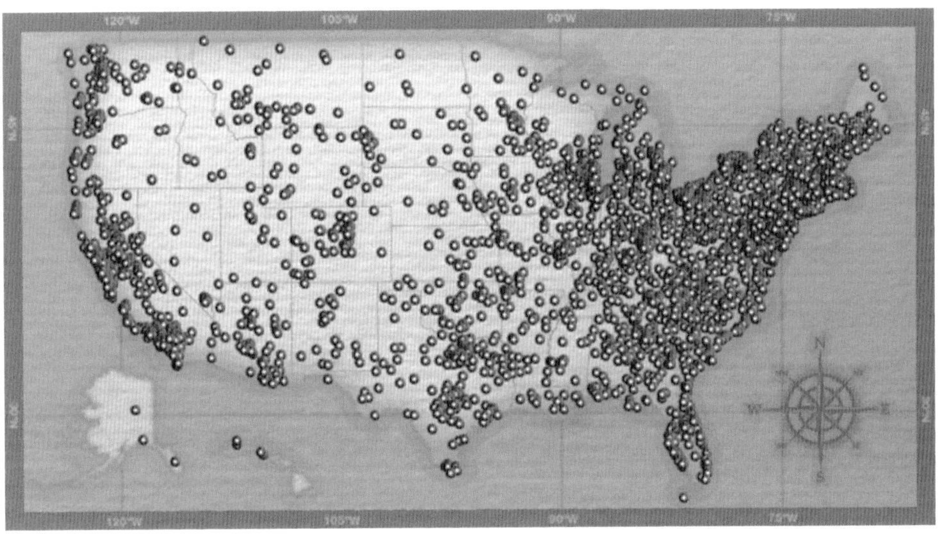